HOW TO WHOLESALE HOUSES FOR HUGE CASH

&

HOW TO WHOLESALE HOUSES FOR HUGE CASH – PART II

(With Contracts Included)

By Ernie Braveboy

Get Your Free Copy of

How to be a Real Estate Millionaire

To Get Your Free Copy, Open the Link

https://ebraveboy_3ee2.gr8.com/

TABLE OF CONTENTS

How To Wholesale Houses for Huge Cash

ERNIE BRAVEBOY

INTRODUCTION

I want to thank you and congratulate you for buying the book, *"How To Wholesale Houses for Huge Profits"*.

This book has lots of actionable information that you can use to wholesale houses for huge profits.

Wholesaling is one of the fastest growing fields in the real estate market today. It appeals to people much in the same way options trading in the stock market does: it comes with vastly minimized risk and does not require you to spend a lot of personal time or money.

The thing is; a good wholesaler who is ready to do what it takes to be good in the field will be great in no time. The good thing is that real estate wholesaling is not a complex field at all; everything about it is simple and organized.

This book will show you how to be an effective wholesaler who can close multiple deals in short periods. It will also show you the fun side of wholesaling, and point out why you should consider taking wholesaling seriously. Let's begin.

Thanks again for buying this book. I hope you enjoy it!

ERNIE BRAVEBOY

Before we can get to a place of discussing how to wholesale houses for profits, it is important to build a strong understanding of what wholesaling entails first. Therefore, if you are a beginner to the field of real estate wholesaling, it is important that you start from the very beginning so that by the time we get to the point of discussing real estate wholesaling, you understand the concept fully. Let's begin.

THE BASICS OF HOUSE WHOLESALING: WHAT EXACTLY IS IT?

Wholesaling is a term house flippers and real estate investors use when talking about the process of joining the dots between buyers and sellers and picking up a check for their efforts. Think of a finder's fee—you may not own the item or asset, but you made it possible for the person who needs it to get it and you make money for making this happen.

When you conduct your wholesaling business in a legal manner, something many investors fail to do and pay dearly for, you can make a lot of money. However, to generate these amounts of money, you have to be smart about wholesaling, and be willing to buckle down and work hard.

With this in mind, what exactly is wholesaling? What does it comprise of?

Rather than go on a winded, technical explanation on what wholesaling is, here is an example to help you fully understand what wholesaling is.

A Wholesaler's Tale: Meet James the Wholesaler

James is a wholesaler. He spends his days looking for the best real estate deals he can find. However, he is not interested in truly getting in to these deals. One day while he is at his favorite coffee shop, he gets a call from Nora, his friend since high school. She wants to sell her house but is not interested in the usual motions of using an agent. She mentions to James that the house could use a few repairs but that she only wants to get rid of it since she does not want to direct any more money into fixing it up.

James decides to have a look at the house. He looks at the condition of the house and notes the repairs that need doing. He offers Nora a price of $75,000 for the house. Nora accepts on the spot. They both sign a purchase agreement. This agreement points that James or any other party he assigns this contract to may buy the property within the next 15 days for a price of $75,000.

James knows of a friend who mentioned in passing that he is an expert in flipping houses and completes several deals every month. Let us call him Joe. James calls Joe and tells him of the house. He makes sure to mention the necessary repairs needed and how much it could be worth after repairs (known as A.R.V or **After Repair Value**). James offers to sell the property to Joe for $80,000.

Joe knows that after fixing the house up, he can make a good profit. He agrees to the price. James and Joe sign an 'assignment contract', which legally means that James is allowing Joe to purchase the property from Nora. James can do this since he signed a purchase agreement with Nora saying that either James or another party could buy the home in 14 days.

How does all this play out? After everything goes through, Joe will pay Nora $75,000 and James will keep the extra $5,000 as a finder's fee. In the real estate industry, this finder's fee is what we call a wholesale fee.

Can you see how potent this is?

James never truly owned the house yet he made $5,000 off it because he acted as the link to Nora and Joe. Such is one of the ways a wholesaler will structure deals and make profits.

You now have an understanding, albeit a general one, of real estate wholesaling. But I know you might be thinking; is this even legal? That's what you will learn next.

THE REAL DEAL WITH WHOLESALING: IS IT ILLEGAL?

You may have noticed that James, the wholesaler, signing both a purchase agreement and an assignment contract with the respective characters in the story.

As far as the legality of real estate wholesaling goes, there is usually a lot of debate surrounding it. Is it legal to wholesale? Some people will say wholesaling is okay, and they are right. Others will say it is not, and will not be wrong either. In truth, there is no black and white answer since the laws on wholesaling differ from state to state.

Staying Within Legal Boundaries

However, as is the cases in every other field, use of sheer common sense can help us determine some illegalities. If, for example, the paperwork is shady, the wholesaling is illegal.

The other thing is that even though laws differ from one state to the next, some hard and fast rules apply everywhere. For instance:

1. It is illegal for anyone who is not a realtor or broker to sell a home for a third party. This is why, if you go back to section 1, an assignment contract had to be in place before Joe, the 3rd party in the story, could become truly involved.

2. It is illegal for a wholesaler to receive a commission. The only people who are privy to a commission are realtors or brokers. If you have it in your contract that you are to

receive a commission for a sale, you are operating outside your legal boundaries and can be subject to prosecution. This brings us to the next part of this chapter.

A Comparison between Legal and Illegal Wholesaling

Here, we shall look at the characteristics of both:

Illegal Flipping and Its Salient Characteristics:

1. Its main intent is usually to defraud somebody, usually the buyer.

2. The buyer is usually unsophisticated and earns a low income.

3. The property sells at a low price and at retail price, or higher.

4. The seller will be unclear on issues surrounding repairs and will do only that which is necessary to cover up defects.

5. There may be collusion with an appraiser to get a price that is higher than retail price.

On the other hand, legal wholesaling is usually open and between two people who are relatively sophisticated. As you may have guessed, honesty is critical and there is strict adherence to legal channels before any transactions happen.

A Legal Wholesale Transaction Will Look Like This:

1. The buyer and the wholesaler will enter a transaction openly with the intention of making a profit

2. There is no fooling or taking advantage of the buyer. There is a level of sophistication as far as he or she is concerned.

3. If the buyer buys the property at a truly low price, its selling price will be considerably below retail price.

4. The wholesaler may choose not to do any repairs to the property. The buyer will determine exactly what needs doing and will estimate both the cost and the A.R.V

5. The buyer will complete his or her own appraisal based on several factors, among them personal experience.

6. There is no lender. As such, there is no bank fraud.

The next question you might have is; what's in it for you? What's so good about wholesaling, which makes it a great income opportunity? That's what you will discover next.

What's In It for You?

What puts off most new investors from getting started on house wholesaling?

For the most part, the fear of failing when dealing with investments that require large inputs of cash or lots of time before maturity is what puts off many people from getting started. Lack of sufficient money, knowledge, and skill, in this case as regards real estate and rehabilitation, plays a big part as well.

If you are new to house flipping, wholesaling is the best place to start. It does not need a lot of startup capital. If anything, apart from asking you to invest your effort, work super hard, and understand real estate law with regard to wholesaling, it does not ask for much else. There is a lot less risk in wholesaling compared to, say, buying a property outright.

Why You Should Wholesale

Here are reasons why you should consider wholesaling

1: You Do Not Need a Lot of Money to Get Started

To get started as a real estate wholesaler, you do not need a large bank account. Putting a house under a purchase contract and then assigning the contract does not require much money. If you are dealing with motivated sellers, the amount of money you need could be as little as $1.

2: You Do Not Have to Take Ownership of the House

When assigning the contracts, you do not take ownership of the property. You are not the party closing the deal and as such, are not in the chain of title at any one time. This eliminates two things: a large part of costs, and most of the risks involved with property that is most likely vacant and requires repairs to make it livable.

3: It Helps You Steadily Learn What Good Deals Truly Are

There is a wholesaling rule that holds up in just about every situation: *if you consistently have trouble selling your wholesale deals, it could be that you are asking too much or lack enough buyers.* A lot of the time, it is the former. With time, you will gain the ability to discern what makes a good deal and what does not.

4: Networking & Building Relationships All Improve the More You Get Into Wholesaling

You will occasionally sell deals to other more experienced investors. Inevitably, you will build relationships with them. If the kinds of deals you sell them are the homerun kind, they will want to be your friend. The benefits of having friendships with such successful investors are many. You could even end up with a mentor who spends years training you on how to be a better house flipper and how to determine A.R.V better.

5: It Is Easy to Wholesale Part-Time and Hold down A Full Time Job at the Same Time

You can wholesale part-time: wholesaling is not too labor intensive. Sure enough, you have to work hard to be familiar with the field, especially while starting out. However, after this, you will spend most of your time marketing and making offers. With time, your screening skills will grow to the point where you do not have to see as many houses because you instantly know which ones will make good deals and which ones will not.

With that understanding, let's now move on to the next bit i.e. wholesaling like pro by avoiding some potential pitfalls.

Well, just because the benefits above look enticing doesn't mean you should go all in on wholesaling without taking into consideration the possible pitfalls. So what is it you need to be aware of if you are to make it big with wholesaling?

A Smart Way to Wholesale: Red Flags to Avoid

We could also have titled this section *"Amateur moves and marketing mistakes too many wholesalers make and that you should avoid as a wholesaler."* It is also a continuation from the previous section.

The trouble with most aspiring wholesalers is that they are impatient. They do not treat the industry with the due respect it deserves or bother to understand the laws. Thus, they flout many of these laws as soon as they start marketing themselves. Equally bad is their disinterest in creating a professional first impression and in so doing, attracting serious buyers.

Here are amateur wholesaling moves you must avoid at all costs especially when making your presence known to others as a house flipper. The reason why most people who attempt wholesaling either come away with nothing, or walk away with a bunch of lawsuits at some point or other, is that they do not put in the necessary work it takes to become as professional and informed as possible.

Amateur Mistake 1: Aimlessly Spamming Social Media Looking for Homes to Wholesale

There are too many social media posts floating in the internet made by people looking for houses to flip. Businesspeople are encouraged to use social media as much as they can. Yet, there is a smart way to go about this.

The bulk of wholesalers who advertise their businesses on social media fail to follow a clear marketing structure that allows them to appear as seriously wholesalers. Take Facebook for example; rather than having pages set up that exclusively cover wholesaling deals, many people will use their personal Facebook accounts that they use to speak on all manner of things—from poodles, to eBay purchases.

This lacks organization, is unprofessional, and defeats any intention you may have of treating your wholesaling as a business. Section 7 gives you general guidelines on how to harness social media and use it to market your business.

Amateur Mistake 2: Putting In Commission Clauses in Your Contract

Section 2 clearly states that it is illegal for anyone who is not a realtor or broker to receive commission on property sold. Too many people do not understand this one, or make sure the commission clause is the first thing on the contract. It is important to understand this: the fee you receive as a wholesaler is a **wholesaler's fee**. You are not privy to a "commission," and including this in your contract is misguided.

While it is true that you do not always have to be caught, it will be a nightmare for you if you someone sues you or takes you to court on an issue surrounding the property deal, and there is mention of this.

Amateur Mistake 3: Having No Purchase Contract and Assignment Contract in Place

This is necessary paperwork. Without this, your wholesaling activity is little more than illegal house flipping, which can get you into serious trouble. Make sure you have these signed by you and the relevant parties.

The above chapter is not meant to scare you but to prepare you for the work ahead to ensure you don't make costly mistakes while wholesaling. To prepare you even the more, the next part will discuss how much work is required if you are to excel as a wholesaler.

EXACTLY HOW HARD DO YOU HAVE TO WORK IN WHOLESALING?

Surely, wholesaling is easy, right, is that not what everybody says about it?

Here is the truth about wholesaling though: **it is hard.** If you are looking for an easy payday, wholesaling is not the field for this.

It is necessary for you to be competent in many things: to be diligent and brave. At any one moment, there will always be an investor with the capacity to outbid you and offer deals far superior to yours. The competition is often fierce and truth be told, there are just too many wholesalers around today to assume it is an easy field.

As a wholesaler, you will often have to work extremely hard to find any deals at all let alone find good deals. You will have to hustle and then hustle some more to stay relevant. A lazy and unmotivated person will usually get nowhere with wholesaling or will break laws that will lead to fines or even jail time.

In short, wholesaling is a business and as is so often the case, any business that succeeds takes a lot of hard work.

How Do Wholesalers Make Good Money?

Successful wholesalers make good money because of this simple reason: they complete multiple deals every passing month. At a standard price of $5,000 for every deal, (this is the average price in as far as wholesale fees go), you do not need too many deals. However, you have to work constantly to know more and more buyers and investors, and what they may be looking for.

To be a good wholesaler who will be around long after most have dropped by the sides, you will need a degree of skill in the following:

1. Understanding the math underlying a good flip and a good rental

2. Keeping your calm in distressed situations and maintaining a civil conversation all through

3. Negotiating with others without taking advantage of them

4. Marketing for those leads that will cost less than the marketing will

5. Cold calling as well as answering phone calls

6. Sales

7. Looking for and finding good deals

8. Estimating ARV (After Repair Value)

9. Estimating the costs of rehabilitation

10. Estimating potential rental fees

What Does All This Mean?

With wholesaling, you will have to put in consistent work. While it is possible to outsource some things, you will still need to be in charge and understand how all of these things work.

To be a wholesaler, you will have to be a hard worker who is not only good at many things, but who also knows how to socialize, reach out to people and respond to them regardless of how bad the emotional climate may be.

Up to this point in life, you may have worn the introvert label with pride. A few things will have to change. There is nothing wrong with being introverted but you will never make any progress by doing the equivalent of sitting by yourself in a full room waiting for others to reach out. You will have to be aggressive.

This section does not serve the purpose of making you rethink your decision to be a wholesaler. Its purpose is to dispel the myth that wholesaling is easy and if anything, it should fill you with hope that you will succeed. How so? Because you now know that most people who get into wholesaling will never succeed since they lack the necessary work ethic. You have a chance to be part of the few who will succeed.

With what we have learnt so far, we will now move on to discussing specific components that determine whether you excel as a wholesaler or not with the first part centering around defining your target area.

DEFINING YOUR TARGET AREA: WHERE DO YOU WANT TO WORK?

As a novice wholesaler, you cannot just assume that you will go wherever possible to find deals. It will be necessary to establish your target area; the area you will focus the bulk of your efforts to finding deals. Many investors who fail to establish a target area often find themselves spending more time than is necessary to lock down good deals. It is also true that this is the most prevalent mistake among most new wholesalers.

You need to focus primarily on one area: your target area. This will help you save time and energy you would otherwise spend scouting a new area and learning about it.

The Target Area

Ideally, your target area should be within a 10-mile radius of where you currently live. Why should you start with where you live? For starters, you probably know the area well. You are familiar with just about everything, down to the side streets. You know the good areas and the bad ones. By starting with your area of residence, you drastically shorten the learning curve. The quicker you learn, the faster you can start making money.

Get a zip code map (visit http://www.usnaviguide.com/) and find 5 zip codes around your residence. Print your map out and draw a circle that fits in the zip codes you choose. This will be your target area. Because it is in your backyard, it is likely that you know everything about it. The next step is to drive the streets and get to know the area even more than you do.

Get to know the names of the streets and the different tracts. Get to know the bad areas as well as what makes them so, and do the same with the good areas. Next, drive to work, the bank or the grocery store, look around and evaluate the area.

Look at old and ugly homes that may be ripe for flipping; take a different route home too. You can also intentionally get lost and work your way back to your place, all in a bid to get to know the area better.

Understand the kinds of houses on each block. Do you have bungalows on one block, stucco structures on another, and wood buildings on yet another block? Is the landscape rock, gravel, grass, desert, or one of large trees? Do you have mostly duplexes or triplexes? Seek to know as much as possible.

Once you've identified your target area, the next part is to find great deals.

FINDING GREAT DEALS AS A WHOLESALER: WHERE DO YOU LOOK?

They say that a wholesaler who lacks a good deal is like a butcher who has no meat: his business is useless, as is any knowledge he may have. To avoid being a meat-less butcher, you must become proficient and increasingly effective in creating a pipeline of good real estate deals.

Why use the term pipeline? Well, your goal as a wholesaler is not to do just one deal at a time. Your goal will be to do multiple deals. However, deals need careful handling, with a degree of patience, until they come to fruition. This could take some time. Thus, the successful wholesaler is consistently filling his or her pipeline with leads and working them through this pipeline.

Here is what to do to get great deals:

1: Look into the MLS

MLS is a collection of all deals currently sold by real estate agents. The competition is severe and as such, it may be difficult to get good deals. Understand that it may be hard to wholesale a home foreclosed by a bank but it is not altogether impossible.

2: Drive for Dollars

What you do here is get into your car and drive around looking for a potential deal. Your goal is to look for property you may consider "depressed." You can spot such property by viewing long grass, windows boarded up, and tarps on the roof, among other things.

3: Network Online

Social media will give you the capacity to reach many people in just one click. You should consider setting up a simple WordPress wholesale site and market yourself from it. It is a smart thing to keep buyers on various destinations too. Once you have your site up and running, link it to Facebook, Instagram, Twitter and even LinkedIn.

4: Learn About Mail Marketing & Be Good At It

You ought to buy real discount bargains well below the market value. It is necessary for a sufficient spread to be present for the end buyer to make some profit. In the event that the price tag, as far as your end goes, is too high, a property you may be unable to dispose of may mess you up.

One of the effective approaches to get decreased costs is via direct mail marketing. While it is true that direct mail marketing can be expensive, it is only so in the event that the property you intend to wholesale is in truly decrepit condition or you are too lazy to mail more than a few people. You could even blend your direct mail marketing efforts with email marketing where you collect email addresses of visitors to your website to make it easier to reach out to them when there is need. Money is in the list; if you are careful with how you collect emails and engage your list appropriately, you can be sure that your marketing campaigns will yield great leads.

5: Attend Real Estate Meetings

These days, every state has a local real estate speculation club. It does not matter what your experience level is: make sure to join your local club. These clubs are usually phenomenal places to discover great discount bargains.

As a beginner wholesaler, wholesaling is not just a way to make some money; it is also a way to gain contacts and learn more about the business. This will all begin with finding deals to buckle down and work on. By using these 5 techniques, you will find good deals in just about every market.

What next after finding great deals? What steps should you take to identify ideal properties? That's what we will discuss next.

THE IDEAL PROPERTY: UTILIZING THE BOARD OF REALTORS & THE DEPOSIT AMOUNT TO GIVE THE HOMEOWNER

What is the ideal property?

If you are advertising properly (the next section mentions how you can go about it effectively), your phone will be constantly ringing. What is the ideal property? Well, the ideal property is that which has a sufficient equity.

Consider this example of a property worth $100,000:

Understanding that the property is worth $100,000, you use your negotiation skills and scale the buying price down to $55,000. You fill out the purchase contract with the homeowner as the seller and you as the buyer.

Assume you already know a good house flipper who likes to make a certain amount of profit on every deal, and you know that you can have him purchase the property in the next week. As a good wholesaler, you will factor in his standard profit amount, as well as other costs such as miscellaneous costs (holding fees and so on) and rehab costs. Adding all these amounts together and subtracting them from the initial $100,000 figure will give you your expected profit amount. (Section 10 will go into depth on this.)

The question here is what are the easiest routes to find such property with sufficient equity?

The Board of Realtors

The Board of Realtors is a good place to start. The contracts on there are wonderfully simple, easy to read and understand, and prepared in such a way that the most unsophisticated homeowner can understand them. As such, it will be very hard for someone to adjudge you to having broken laws and taken advantage of a homeowner.

Call your Board of Realtors and ask if they sell contracts to public folk. Most states will have a Board of realtors that has no issues making contracts available to the public.

The Sales Contract

The first line will be reserved for the buyer's name. This is where you put your name. Below, will be a space for "and/assigns"- fill in the necessary information here. This will allow you to assign your contract to the prospective buyer, such as another house flipper.

The Deposit Amount

To make the contract binding, it will be necessary to leave a deposit with the present homeowner. You do not have to hurt your wallet: wholesalers occasionally leave deposit amounts as low as $1. A $25 deposit is usually sufficient. This way, if wholesaling the property becomes difficult, you will not be too much out of pocket.

Surely, a $25 deposit is too low to be taken up?

Actually, it is not. Simply put it like this, *"We usually give a $25 deposit and then make sure we close in X number of* *days (say, 50 days)."* This powerful statement is one that will always meet sellers' expectations. The only reason homeowners will reject your proposed deposit amount is because you present it all wrong. Express yourself with confidence. Once you can do this, and especially attach a specific timeframe that works for you, it is very easy to sell yourself to homeowners.

Next, we will discuss the process of wholesaling in 8 simple steps.

WHOLESALING IN 8 EASY STEPS: THE GENERAL FORMAT TO FOLLOW WHEN WHOLESALING

A successful wholesaling process typically takes 8 steps, in the order below. By following the steps below, you will successfully wrap up deals and make a profit, and do so entirely within the law.

Step 1: Marketing

This is the most vital bit in your wholesaling business. You get your business going by marketing. You need to market your business to get deals. Your marketing plan, to be truly effective, will need to comprise of a combination of social media, broadcasting, and networking.

Step 2: Make Calls & Respond to Mail

Once you start getting responses because of your marketing efforts, you need to start capturing and analyzing all the responses. After capturing the responses, the next bit is to qualify them. You will do this by tracking the mode with which you received the responses with the examples of bandit signs, e-mail, direct mail, social media, and telephone.

Step 3: Inspect Your Property

You need to understand the condition of the property and as such, its value. You will need to evaluate its renovation, if it requires it. You will get there by picking up as much information on the property as you can. You need to conduct a thorough inspection to get this information.

Understand that as a wholesaler, you do not have to give exact figures. Your job is to get the absolute best estimate, in the ballpark, and in so doing, ensure your numbers make sense. This is only possible if you fully understand the state of your property.

Step: Negotiating the Deal

Perhaps you are familiar with the saying *"You do not find a good deal, you make one."* It will be very rare for you to get a call from somebody who is willing to sell the property at 70% of the A.R.V, minus the cost of repairs. Just about every seller will want to get top dollar for the home. It will be up to you to get the best possible price and in so doing, create a win-win situation for both seller and yourself. You will have to develop your negotiation skills. As they become better, your deals will get better as well.

Step 5: Get it all Under Contract

Once you have agreed to a deal with the seller, you will need to have him or her sign a contract. It will be advisable that you learn a lot about the legal implications of transactions as well as the legal paperwork. It will be necessary for you to educate yourself on entity structuring as well as buying and sales contracts. On top of this, you need to know what to do with these contracts once you have them signed.

Step 6: Identify a Buyer

Once you have the deal under control (that is under contract), and you know you have a great deal, the next step is to advertise your deal. You can make calls to the renovators you meet in your networking groups, post the deal online using such outlets as craigslist; the list goes on and on.

Step 7: Conduct an Assignment of Contract

Once you have come to an agreement with the buyer, you will need to transfer your responsibilities and rights in the contract to the buyer. You will do this via an assignment of contact (you will have the buyer sign an assignment contract.)

Step 8: Closing Your Deal & Cashing the Check

The deal-closing bit also goes by settlement. When closing, you will sign the appropriate documents and then cash your check.

Here is a tip for you: always ask your sellers for a testimonial. A collection of testimonials will go a long way in marketing your business.

Next, let's discuss about how much to offer.

THE OFFER: HOW MUCH SHOULD YOU OFFER?

The one thing you should understand about wholesaling is that you will only make money when others are making money. Thus, you have to come up with the right offer. The amount cannot be too high or too low as this will hurt you financially in one way or the other.

Just how much should you offer?

Going by the paragraph above and understanding that you will only make money when somebody else makes money too, you will have to reverse engineer the entire dynamic. If you are selling to another house flipper, he or she will have to make a profit; otherwise, he or she will not be willing to buy the property from you. The key is to understand what they want. Even better, understand what their margins are.

Constructing Your Offer Based On ARV

Everything begins with the ARV (After Repair Value). The key is to have this number in mind. Once you do, start working backwards:

1. How much does the person you are selling to, if he or she is a flipper, aim to make on the deal?

2. What are the rehab costs?

3. What are the miscellaneous costs, such as holding costs and others?

4. How much profit do you want to make?

Now that you know the ARV figure, you will understand the highest amount you can pay on the deal.

It will look a bit like this:

Your Offering Price = A.R.V – The Total of the (Bulleted) Areas Above

Look at this example:

Jack is a wholesaler. He finds a property and because he has some experience checking out distressed property and determining its value, he determines that the value is $190,000. He knows a good flipper; he also knows that the flipper usually makes a $30,000 profit on most flips. Jack does more research, walks through the property, and checks the condition of every facility. He determines that the miscellaneous costs (commissions, closing costs, and the like) will come to just under $25,000.

Jack calls up a contractor and walks him through the property. The contractor determines that the rehab costs will come to about $40,000. Jack also knows that he wants a wholesale fee of $5,000.

This is how John determines his offering price:

Offering Price = $190,000 - $30,000 - $25,000 - $40,000 - $5,000

The price he comes up with = $89,000 (or a bit less than this)

How exactly do you keep abreast with all these numbers?

To begin with, none of this is as hard as it may appear. If you can perform basic math and have access to a generous amount of paper, it is easy to figure most of this out. It helps if you love mathematics. However, if you do not like math and are uninterested in spending thousands of dollars on a personal coach, consider a wholesale calculator. Bigpockets has a spectacular wholesale calculator you can find on:

A wholesaling calculator, such as the BiggerPockets.com one, lets you quickly determine your Maximum Allowable Offer for every potential wholesale deal. Most of these calculators are easy to use and they walk you through relevant questions in a systematic format.

We've been talking a lot about ARV but haven't really discussed how to determine the ARV. The next part will discuss just that.

MATTERS REGARDING ARV: DETERMINING ARV

The previous section mentioned the use of wholesale calculators to help you determine a proper offering price. However, the offering price will be heavily dependent on the ARV. No wholesale calculator will determine the ARV for you, and the ARV is the most vital number in the entire process of finding a good offer especially given that you will subtract every single figure from this particular one. Therefore, you must ensure you have an accurate ARV value.

How Do You Determine The ARV?

Multiple methods exist, but they all revolve around one principle: *A house will be worth roughly what similar local houses have gone for in recent times.*

Of course, it will be important to determine just how close a property has to be to qualify as local. If a property was sold 20 miles away, it may not be close enough. Other factors should play a part in determining ARV; a sold 4-bedroom house will not be similar enough to a 2-bedroom house you want to wholesale. A home was sold in an awful condition is not similar to a well-kept home.

While it is highly unlikely to find an identical home sold recently, you need to get as close as possible to recently sold homes to determine an accurate ARV. Consider every factor you think will hold some weight. Did the recently sold home have 2 bathrooms, while yours has one? Did the other home have 500 square foot less of space compared to your own? Use all these factors to determine the ARV.

An Easy Way to Determine ARV: Using Real Estate Agents

You do not have to hire the services of one: just ask intelligent questions. A lot of them are usually glad to talk about real estate, a subject they love, and they have lots of data as far as recently sold homes go. However, consider that there are agents who will not want freely give advice they consider professional. Find a way to make it worth for such ones.

One of the ways you can do this is drop them unworkable leads that hold the potential to make them some money. This will forge strong friendships that will be beneficial for you.

Once you have the ARV, let's now focus on how to talk to the seller to make an irresistible offer.

TALKING TO THE SELLER & MAKING AN OFFER: A PROCESS

After covering the steps outlined in the previous sections, the time will be ripe to put your selling hat on and make an offer.

Talking Up the Seller and Presenting an Offer

You will need to sell yourself while "devaluing" the property at the same time. This works to make the homeowner realize that the deal you are offering is a superb deal. In addition, you are offering to make a purchase "as is, where is, and with no inspection required" (this means with no need to perform any rehab measures). This means regardless of how broken down the property is, you will not need the seller to put up any rehab or repair costs.

Sell the Homeowner the Idea That You Are Taking Risks

Make sure the seller understands that you are assuming all the risk in the deal and not only are you doing this, you intend to pay cash quickly (give them a period you will operate in). You need to put forth an offer that is hard to refuse.

Few people are interested in paying repair fees of fixing up their house before they make a sale. Most times, all they want it for the house to stop being their business anymore and to have some money in the bank to show for their sale. Convince the seller that you are indeed helping him or her out.

The "Inspection Contingency" & Using It to Get the Best Deal

Traditional purchase agreements usually have an inspection contingency built into them. This means the potential buyer, which is you in this case, may back out if you do not like the look of things post-inspection.

You backing out of the deal is a massive hassle for the homeowner. The process of finding someone else to jump through all the hoops of the purchasing process is a taxing one.

Consider this three-point scenario:

- You are empowered to back out at any time

- The house is broken down to the level that it is not immediately livable and requires rehab.

- The homeowner cannot afford these repairs

A typical home inspection process is capable of tying up a house for 2 weeks or more. What is more, most traditional deals will usually take up to 45 days to close. This will mean the seller will not see any money for 2 months. In addition to this, it may be necessary to pay for house repairs just to get an interested buyer. This is quite unappealing to the homeowner. Use all of this to press your point.

An example of approaching a buyer who refuses to budge below $110,000:

"I understand you want $110K for the house. However, I am countering at $79K. Here is why: I can pay you cash on

Wednesday next week and I will buy your house "as is, where is, with no inspection". This way, you will have no repair worries, and neither do you have to go through all the hassle of inspection. You will literally have cash on hand by Wednesday evening."

Next, we will discuss how to close deals.

CLOSING THE FIRST WHOLESALE DEAL: 3 TIPS TO MAKE IT MOVE FASTER

Here are 3 tips to help you close a deal fast:

Tip 1: It Helps To "Mind Your Due Diligence"

What exactly does this mean? This means you do whatever it takes to become as educated on the subject of wholesaling as possible. Read as many related pamphlets and books as you could. Attend as many seminars as is possible. If there are any networking events you can attend, make sure you are among the first people to arrive. It helps a lot if you have a relationship with experienced hands in the game. Do whatever it takes to become relevant in the lives of experienced house flippers.

Do you know the biggest reason why most beginners fail to close even one deal? It is because they skipped this step and dove straight into trying to find and close deals. Before you do anything, take care of this stage. Give yourself several weeks to become truly familiar with the field. Those few weeks may be the difference between decades of mediocrity or success.

Tip 2: A Buyers List Is Important

A buyers list is not as hard to create as you may think. All you need to do is be a proactive person. Make sure you collect the contact information of everyone you meet, whether in wholesaling-based meet-ups, or otherwise. Record this information carefully. It will not hurt you to show some professional flair and give out business cards to people. Not everybody will call you; however, if you give out enough of them, someone will eventually pick up the phone and dial your number.

Tip 3: Make Sure To Target Motivated Sellers

What is the best technique to reach motivated sellers? It is not picking up the phone and cold calling; neither is it spamming their social media handles. The technique that really pulls the motivated sellers away from the rest of the lot is direct mail. While simple, there is directness to this method that appeals to serious sellers.

Which people will qualify as motivated sellers and thus, your primary targets? Look for delinquent taxpayers, absentee owners, owners of property who do not live in the county or state, and people with homes whose foreclosure date is near. Ideally, look for "distressed property," as this book so aptly pointed to in an earlier section.

Cash Buyers: How Do You Find Cash Buyers Quickly?

Your goal as wholesaler is to generate money and at the same time, dispose of property with as much speed as possible. This is necessary so you can focus on getting even more deals and building your portfolio quickly.

Knowing this, whom are you going to sell your property to?

The best kind of buyer will be the "cash buyer." You have likely heard of this term before. While it is a bit of a buzzword that too many gurus like to toss around, it is indeed a real thing.

Who Is a Cash Buyer?

A cash buyer will be a buyer who can pay cash for the property. This is all quite simple, or so it appears. Understand that this cash does not have to be their cash. A lot of the time, cash buyers will use hard money or private money to close a deal. The point of all this is this: The buyer does not have to go through the hassle of a lengthy loan process that is prone to rejection anyway. It is 100% guaranteed that when the day to wire the money comes, the sale should go through.

Usually, most of your cash buyers will be house flippers. However, there will be the occasional real estate developer as well. When it comes to cash buyers, the key thing to understand is that everybody is looking for a good deal these days. If you make a habit of offering good deals, you will not run out of cash buyers.

Your ideal buyers list, for everything mentioned in this book, will comprise of 100% cash buyers. If this is not possible, ensure most of the people in it are cash buyers. With this said, there is a lot of hype on finding cash buyers. There are many thousand-dollar programs floating around. Many of those programs are overpriced and overhyped. Save some money and follow the following advice:

Cash buyers are easy to find. However, they are only easy to find after you have done everything else right. If you do so, you will quickly discover that cash buyers are everywhere.

How do you find them though?

Craigslist is a good option. The ads you put on there are free. Paying for a newspaper ad is also an option. However, one of the greatest ways that always works is to ask a real estate agent to provide you with a list of every home within a radius of 20 miles that was a cash sale. This is easy data to get. After doing this, perform some public searching of records to know who bought those homes and then send them mail or cold call them.

After closing the deal, what next? Let's find out.

POST-DEAL ACTIVITY & GETTING PAID

If you do everything else in this book and do it well, the next logical step is to get paid. Everything else leads to this. Getting paid will mean you can further expand your wholesaling business. It will also mean a lot as far as having some extra money goes.

You have taken the time to learn as much as you can on wholesaling. You have worked to find the best deals. You have done a thorough job of assessing the property and determining the ARV. You have worked on your math and you know how much you will offer the seller to make a profit on the deal.

You have done what it takes to attract cash buyers to you and build a sizable buyers list. Everything is ok and all that is remaining is to have the money wired to your bank account. What do you need to know about this process? What can you expect and how do you move forward?

Getting paid

This may well be the easiest and most straightforward process in this entire package of process. This is because there will not be much for you to do. All you need is to get all the information to the title company. This is inclusive of every contract you have signed. After this, you sit back and wait. If you are in a state that does not use Title Companies and instead uses attorneys, you will get the information to the closing attorney; they should take care of everything else, if they are competent.

Try working with a title company or attorney familiar with wholesaling. Too many of them are unfamiliar with it. If you are unsure of the best one for you, ask some local wholesalers to help you out.

At the end, the seller will get the money promised. The cash buyer is going to get a superb deal. As for you, well, you will become a little richer.

What are you going to do with your money though? Will you buy a new car? Will you finally overhaul that dated wardrobe you own?

All this is ok but if you are a smart wholesaler, you will view this money as an investment and will make sure to channel it into your marketing budget so that you keep a full pipeline. A single deal will not transform your life. However, creating a good pipeline that consistently delivers good deals certainly will change it.

With that in mind, let's now discuss some general guidelines to keep in mind while going about your business as a wholesaler.

GENERAL ADVICE: THE KINDS OF WHOLESALERS YOU DO NOT WANT TO BE

You do not want to be any of the following wholesalers:

1: The Miss-Informed Wholesaler

This wholesaler is the kind of person who refuses to be smart while looking for deals, especially when building a buyers list. Why do new wholesalers think they can skip doing the actual work and get a $100 buyers list from "a source" that will forever transform their lives? This mistake is one often made despite being one of the more foolish mistakes.

To build a good buyers list, you have to put in the work by actively searching for cash buyers and motivated sellers. You need to build your contacts in an organic manner; this requires time and effort.

2: The "I Am Not Too Sure I Want To Be A Wholesaler" Wholesaler

This fellow gives a story like this: "Last week was absolute bliss. Seriously, it was great! I caught up with 5 of my friends and there was so much to gossip about we talked for 8 hours straight. Can you believe we even forgot all about eating during that period? We did not even have water. All this time, my phone was ringing off the hook; some cash buyers who picked the absolute worst time to call. Well, I put it on mute so that I could call them after I was done gossiping with my friends. After all, what are we without our friends?"

3: The Cheap Wholesaler

This sort of wholesaler will usually have a story that goes like this: "I sent out over 5,000 letters last month. I only got 5 calls, and none of them were from motivated sellers, if sellers at all. Their replies all went like this, "I was about to throw the piled up letters in the bin when I saw your letter. I only picked it up because I thought it was a bill. I am sorry but I am not selling my property." Well, I figure next month will be a better month for me."

You have to do more than just send letters. You need to get into your car and drive around the neighborhood looking at property. It will do you good to pick up the phone and cold call. Make sure to cultivate relationships with real estate agents, other wholesalers, and house flippers. Spread your net as wide as you can and build as many relationships as possible. The more you know, the more likely you are to close a good deal.

HOW TO WHOLE SALE HOUSES FOR HUGE CASH

PART II

INTRODUCTION

I want to thank you and congratulate you for buying the book, "how to wholesale houses for huge cash (part 2 with contracts included)".

This book has a lot of actionable and authoritative information on how to wholesale houses for huge cash.

You've always wanted to dip your business feet in real estate, to strike it big in the field, and through it, fashion a better life for yourself. You know you can do it because not only do you have the requisite work ethic necessary to survive in what is often a cutthroat business, you are willing to do whatever it takes and learn whatever you need to learn to become a successful real estate investor. Nevertheless, one thing has consistently shut the real estate investment door in your face: your lack of funds.

If you can relate to this, you may be in luck; the phenomenon of wholesaling may very well be the solution to your lack of funds problem. If you're willing to work hard and smart, you can succeed in real estate without necessarily having much in the way of money.

This book will guide you through wholesaling. It'll teach you everything you need to know to not only become a great wholesaler but one who stays on the right side of the law without necessarily muffling his or her ambition and aggression in getting business done.

The content in this book seeks to build on what the first book cover. By the end of this book, you should be a much more complete wholesaler in terms of business mentality and acuity.

Thanks again for buying this book. I hope you enjoy it!

WHOLESALING 101: WHOLESALING AND REAL ESTATE IN GENERAL

Book 1 introduced you to being a wholesaler. This section and the rest of this book will build on what you learned in book one so that, by the time you turn the last page of this book, you will become a more refined wholesaler.

What better place to start than at the one constant element present in just about all things, real estate wholesaling included, *the element of change.*

Adapting To Change: Technology and Its Stronghold on People

In recent years, people have been moving away from desktop PCs to laptops, and from laptops to tablets and smartphones. This can only mean that compared to 5 years ago, today, people are getting their information from different avenues. They are also relying a lot more heavily on the internet and social media for their "information fix" than they have been at any other point in time. It's for this reason that you should:

Start with old school methods but a transition to digital platforms and with time, lean heavily on them:

When you first start out, I encourage (as most experts in this field will tell you) to begin with older methods of finding properties and self-marketing. Here, think of strategies such as driving in search of houses or putting up bandit signs to let the neighborhood know of your presence (beware that the latter will also let the authorities know of your presence.) Book 1 recommends this, for a fact.

Doing this (using old-school methods) is necessary because of it:

1. Gives you firsthand practical experience

2. Toughens your hide against rejections and failed deals

3. Makes you get better at prospecting motivated buyers and ideal properties

4. Being on the ground where you deal with people directly and take people you think will be valuable to your development for drinks and such is a good way to build your network and market yourself.

However, to really grow, you have to be increasingly less traditional and more digitally oriented because in a vastly digitized world, going digital is the best way to reach more people and find more houses to wholesale or sell.

Therefore, you should consider modern marketing avenues such as:

1. **Twitter:** Set up a Twitter account that broadcasts to everyone that you are a wholesaler. Getting re-tweets and mentions will lead to great exposure.

2. **Facebook:** Like Twitter, set up a Facebook account, complete with images and multiple relevant posts, that shows your wholesaling intent.

3. **Set up a Site:** Set up a simplistic blog or website that markets your business and perhaps display some relevant ads there. This way, you make money twofold: by wholesaling and revenue from paid ad clicks. However, don't overdo with the ads, as you could easily make your website/blog to look less professional.

By going digital, you instantly cease being just local; you become global and everyone around the world has a chance to know you and make deals with you. By moving onto social media and the internet, you expose yourself to the world and get a chance to grow your brand exponentially.

Can you see why this is powerful? To make matters even better, social media and internet use will work passively for you most of the time; however, you still need to update your footprint online and track what people are saying about your business and brand.

With a bit of basic on what it takes to be a successful wholesaler in the current times, let's now tackle something else; how to become a wholesaler even if you have no money.

CAN YOU ACTUALLY WHOLESALE WITH ZERO MONEY DOWN?

In just about every article or piece on wholesaling, you will see people marketing their service by telling you that you can begin wholesaling with absolutely no money down. No matter how you look at it, this looks too good to be true. Still, the people who tell you that you can wholesale with no money down repeat the same thing because it's not entirely untrue. Let us get to it and debunk this if it indeed deserves debunking.

Can you wholesale with no money down?

The correct answer is yes... and no.

As you saw in Book 1's story of James the wholesaler, it is indeed possible to wholesale with no money down. However, this book has to admit that the story of James glossed over and overly simplified something, the part where James gets the call from Nora, high school friendship notwithstanding. The truth is:

You have to spend so as not to spend:

This subtitle is likely to sound like a riddle- that is not intentional. Let us go back to James example. Would you say James ended up being a serious prospect to Nora because he stayed inactive and idle? The answer is no, and you cannot really chalk it up to the two were high school friends. Nora was looking to make a sale (and make money) not to catch up with an old friend. She had to do what was best for business.

At its core, wholesaling is a marketing game. It, therefore, makes sense that the best wholesalers are also the best marketers. If there ever were a hard and fast marketing rule, the rule would be that marketing is rarely free and the more effective it is, the more costly it is.

Let us examine James' situation, and just how he may have been able to not only have Nora seek him out, but have Joe as a business friend and thus, be able to finalize a wholesale deal in a matter of days.

At first, James may have had nothing to go by. His portfolio was only stacked in his imagination, he lacked any clientele, and he likely did not know Joe. To get somewhere, James may have had to be very proactive. He may have:

1. Fueled his car and scouted his immediate neighborhood looking for properties he could start with. James may have advanced his scouting so that he scoured the entire county in search of properties on sale and in an attempt to grow his client base and portfolio. Fuel costs money and driving around like that certainly takes up time. James could have easily used this time to make money from a conventional avenue such as working overtime at his day job.

2. James may have "interned" with a seasoned wholesaler where he had to pay the said wholesaler a fee to show him the ropes as well as show him how to close deals quickly and make valuable friends in the business. The wholesaling veteran may have been kind enough to introduce him to one or two contacts so that he could get started.

3. James may have spent money on books—such as the money you've spent on this book—to be able to learn all he could on wholesaling and what he needed to do to break the ground. He, of course, had to act on the knowledge he gained from the books, but purchasing the books or brochures was the first step.

4. James could very well have paid an experienced wholesaler for the service of an introduction to some clients or just their phone numbers, something many aspiring wholesalers do. Granted, it's not quite as organic as what this book teaches you, but there is nothing illegal about it and if you can, you should go this route as well.

There are dozens of scenarios that James could have put himself in to advance himself, but the constant element is that he had to spend some money to get ahead. You are now in a position to understand what the "yes...and no" answer points to. Can you wholesale with no money down? Yes, you can...but you really cannot.

Next, we will be discussing how to become a lean wholesaler.

BECOMING EXTRAORDINARY: MOLDING YOURSELF INTO A LEAN WHOLESALER

At this point, you are more than familiar with the standard definition of the wholesaler as a professional. Let's take that understanding a step further and shed more light on the unique group of real estate investors called wholesalers. Beyond the standard definition, who are they really, at least with regard to other real estate investors?

Wholesalers are real estate investors whose talent and reputation is too often overshadowed by hasty, less-experienced wholesalers who ultimately give the whole group a poor reputation.

The 2 Kinds of Wholesalers

Going by this definition, it is apparent that there are two kinds of wholesalers. The first group, the group that means business, is that of the out-and-out professionals, and the 2nd group is that of those who cannot be bothered enough to understand the intricacies of the wholesaling business, have no regard for ethics and structure, and often end up in trouble with the law.

This section of this guide shows you what you need to do to be an outstanding wholesaler with the utmost professionalism.

What Makes a Phenomenal Wholesaler?

The answer to this question is simple: to be considered a phenomenal wholesaler, you need to have ALL the traits of a real estate pro, combined. What does this mean?

1. A great wholesaler needs to be a rehab guru (one who buys subpar property, fixes it up, and sells it off).

2. He or she needs to be an expert in the ways of the landlord (one whose specialty is purchasing property to rent out).

3. He or she needs to be a real estate agent (one who looks out for and finds properties for the rehab gurus and landlords).

All of this looks too tall an order to meet especially if you take it at face value. What this means, however, is that to become complete as a wholesaler, you need to be familiar with all, and combine all the three mindsets. This section is not asking you to become a landlord, a property rehab expert, or a real estate agent even though the latter has multiple similarities to what it means to be a wholesaler. This section is simply asking you to seek to understand what each deals with, goes through, looks out for, and seeks to accomplish in multiple scenarios.

These three individuals have unique traits that allow them to succeed.

1. A rehab guru has the uncanny ability to visualize what a property will look like after fixing up, and what its value will be relative to its present, unrepaired state.

2. The landlord has the ability to view the property and determine if it will give him value for money when rented out.

3. A real estate agent is great at finding "diamonds in the rough."

What can you do to merge all three mindsets into one? Two things:

1. You need to learn as much as you can. It is important that you read as much material as you can on all three kinds of investors. If you can attend seminars, do it. If you can talk to seasoned professionals in all three real estate professions, set up appointments with them and follow up on any calls you make; few things beat listening to seasoned people talk about their professions. They often provide deep insight, which they often take for granted. They are also very happy to share since most people rarely ask for the insight—they mostly focus on money.

2. Seek to experience what they deal with as closely and as first hand as you can. Try your hand at wholesaling rentals and residential properties alike. Learn until you become or almost become who they are. In the acting circles, they call this sort of intense study an embodiment of values and, most importantly, experience, as "method," as in "method acting." Seek to become a "method wholesaler" who knows the ins and outs of all three real estate professions.

The True Skill of a Phenomenal Wholesaler

What have we been building up to and what is the ultimate skill you will be looking to develop by doing all this? Let us have a bit of a preamble before getting to this:

Real estate is risky; to transition from merely making money to being successful, you will have to take multiple risks. Some properties will not convince you wholesomely even when the potential is there to see. If you are to survive and thrive in this business, you cannot pass up on every deal that does not promise 100% profits. Thus, taking risks and venturing into the unknown will be your reality as a wholesaler.

By seeking to combine all three mindsets, you will minimize your proneness to mistakes even as you take risks. You will get infinitely better at taking educated risks. Thus, the "true" skill you will be after is that of taking an educated risk. How is this viable?

Well, with so much knowledge picked up and firsthand information on what to expect with different property types and scenarios, you will often KNOW what a property offers and what it does not. This very quality may see you thrive in the business while so many others pull out.

Now that you understand the mindset and skills you should strive to build to be a successful wholesaler, in the next chapter, our focus will be on finding deals.

FINDING DEALS: ACTIONABLE STRATEGIES YOU CAN USE TO FIND DEALS QUICKLY

This section builds on a similarly titled section/chapter in Book 1 and offers more insight on how you can acquire wholesale deals, especially if you are just starting out. It will do you good to combine the material here with what we covered in Book 1.

The best way to find deals is to know what you are looking for in the first place. This should be your starting point; everything else should progress from there. With that in mind, here are several strategies you can use to find properties:

1) Aggressively search the classified ads be they online or offline. Do not be too general in your search, as this will then mean that you have to search through a lot of chaff to get something that is ideal for you. You should streamline your search by including such terms as "needs rehab work," "owner carries," "urgent sale," "looking for quick sale," "investor special," and the like. Such terms are also handy in getting you to come across "motivated sellers," a subject covered in detail in the next section.

2) Advertise your services. Often times, the best way to do this is via social media. If you have a good Twitter or Facebook following, it helps a lot to advertise on these platforms and encourage your friends to spread the word. If you want to go a step further, consider paid ads on other people's websites and blogs (pay per click being especially viable.) The latter may cost you considerable

sums of money, but it may get you started in ways that would have otherwise been impossible without spending. How should your ad look like? Well, make it brief: succinct. Something like *"I am a cash buyer looking for houses"* with your phone number below will do.

3) Seek out seasoned real estate agents and realtors and establish a relationship with them, do them a favor of some sort so you get their attention, or intern for them for a while. Why bother with this? Because real estate agents and realtors understand real estate circles and know motivated sellers who should be your number 1 target as a wholesaler. The idea is to seek an introduction to such people or simply their contacts. It is not quite as organic as the other strategies here, but it works well and helps you begin business faster.

4) Use car magnets and bandit signs. These can display such messages as "I buy houses and pay cash." To be honest, these are not what we would call "entirely legal." However, the most you will face from the authorities are phone calls demanding that you take them down. By then, you should have made some headway. Bandit may not be the most professional or best way to find houses, but they are extremely effective at getting you through to people who are not technologically shrewd or are uninterested in searching the internet for buyers.

5) Attend your local real estate club meetings. While there's no guarantee that you will get deals directly from doing so, such meetings provide you with the opportunity to

network with wholesalers and buyers, which may ultimately help you greatly.

As you scout for deals, it is important that you understand a phenomenon referred to as a 'motivated seller' phenomenon.

THE MOTIVATED SELLER PHENOMENON: UNDERSTANDING WHAT A MOTIVATED SELLER IS AND HOW TO FIND ONE

The section above mentions that finding motivated sellers should be your number one priority. As one who is new or relatively new to wholesaling, this rings very true. However, let us begin by noting that the real estate circles vastly overuse the term "motivated seller" to a point where too many people have little or no idea of what it means anymore. So, what does "a motivated seller" mean? What makes somebody a motivated seller?

Recognizing the Motivated Seller

More often than not, the motivated seller draws motivation from two primary factors: ***money*** and ***time***. Often, the two overlap to a point of being the same thing. If you have ever been in a situation where you needed money urgently and needed it quickly or some undesirable developments would occur, then you understand what this means.

The motivated seller is often looking to sell his or her house within a short period to both make money and wash his or her hands off the house fast. A lot of the time, the house itself is just as much of a problem as the lack of money. We could thus say that a motivated seller is one who is hard-pressed to sell a house quickly and make money off it within as short a period as possible.

How do you recognize prospective motivated sellers?

Here are several factors to keep an eye on for when determining a motivated seller. The factors here do not cover the whole range of motivated seller situations but they are by far the most common and you will rarely go wrong with them:

1) The seller's home is either in or near foreclosure. Looming foreclosure completely changes the seller's landscape when it comes to making a purchase. There is no time to let sentiment get in the way of a sale (think something like overpricing the house because the seller's personal valuation of it far outweighs what its really worth.) There is no time to fix up what needs fixing up so that the seller can get a better price for it. The only way forward is to sell off the house as fast as possible. A seller facing foreclosure will usually be very willing to sell it off at a far lower price than he or she otherwise would without the foreclosure pressure.

2) There has been a death in the family and family members are looking to offload the house quickly. Many houses in the U.S go into the market immediately after the owner passes on. This is perhaps because the family is seeking to raise funds to balance out some debt the deceased accrued or it could be that moving forward, the maintenance costs will be too steep and thus unmanageable. It could also be that the family wants to move to a new neighborhood. Whatever the reasons are,

you will often find that the sellers deliberately underprice the house to move it on quickly.

Here are several more factors:

1) There is a divorce, which compels the quick sale of the house. This is often very common since the house's value is often part of the alimony calculations.

2) The seller has made a few terrible investment decisions and he or she needs quick money to fix his or her mess.

3) The seller has built a new house and has not been able to sell off the old house yet.

4) The seller is looking to get rid of a vacation home since he or she feels there is little reason to keep owning it.

5) A job transfer that compels the seller to move to another locality and thus, he/she has to sell off the old house.

6) The seller has already moved and is impatient to sell off the old house quickly to make some money and avoid maintenance costs of a house he or she is not living in anymore.

Assuming that you find a motivated seller, you will undoubtedly need to see the house, as this is the first step to closing a deal. Let's discuss that next.

GOING TO SEE THE SELLER'S HOUSE: WHERE TO LOOK AND WHAT TO YOU LOOK AT

Visualize this. You have had the good fortune of receiving a call from a motivated buyer, and she wants to know if you can begin looking at her house so she can sell it off immediately. Like the smart wholesaler you are, you have told her to wait until you have visited her house and conducted a thorough inspection, something that should not take too long to do.

After agreeing to arrive at her house tomorrow at 8.00 am, you hang up and begin working on the necessary purchase and assignment contracts. There's one kink though, this is your very first wholesale deal. You have never visited a potential seller's house before with the intention of selling it off.

In short, you are not sure what to do. So what do you do? How can you make sure you conduct the inspection right so that you can make the right assessments, peg an appropriate price to the house, and ensure that at the end of the day, you make a profit? That's what we will be discussing in this chapter.

What You Should Do

Here are the several steps to take to ensure you do a thorough job of looking at the house:

1) Make a good first impression, which means show some manners by warmly introducing yourself to the seller.

2) Once done with the introductions, ask the seller if she minds if you take some pictures. If you are truly keen on getting off on the right foot, you need to take pictures so that you can use them to crunch the numbers at your own pace later. There will come a time when you will not need to take any pictures when you will be able to estimate property value just by looking it over, but this knack is one you will have to build with experience. For now, pictures will be necessary.

3) Take many pictures, as many as 50-100 pictures. That sounds like a lot. However, it is vital that you take that many pictures. As a new wholesaler, you may not have the knack to estimate any rehabilitation costs as well as property price in the short time you are on your seller's property. You may also not be comfortable with calculating rehab costs in front of the seller. Having lots of pictures allows you to take your time, once you are back at your place, and make the right estimates based off of the large amounts of "evidence" at your disposal. When it comes to the picture:

a) Take several angles of the sides, exterior front, the back, roof, garage, sidewalk, driveway, and a couple of the street view each way.

b) With the interior, it will be wise to shoot multiple angles of every room in the house, ensuring to photograph the roof as well as the floor.

c) You will need to photograph the basement or utility room. Shoot from several angles here. In addition, you need to take pictures of the electrical panel, furnace, and hot water tank. Simply put, we are saying that you should take pictures of just about everything except the seller herself.

d) When shooting the pictures, have the seller accompany you. Ask her lots of probing questions all while keeping yourself busy with the camera. Your being busy will put her at ease and remove the interrogation aspect from the entire prospect. All your questions should lead to finding a definitive answer on the owner's primary motivation for selling. Remember that any information you get will help you negotiate the deal.

When done inspecting the property, and you have determined that it indeed meets your criteria, tell the seller that you will get back to her with an offer the next day. Always make sure to give her a specific date lest she seeks out someone else (when you gain more experience, you may well be able to make an offer on the spot).

Head back to your office and calculate your offer. If you're not well experienced with determining amounts, let this be your guide.

Your offer (also known as a ***maximum allowable offer***), will see you take 70% off the value of the property AFTER repairs, and then subtract the rehab costs and desired assignment fee from it. The final figure will be your ideal amount to offer: the ***Maximum Allowable Offer.*** Use this formula until you are comfortable making deals on the spot.

As you work towards giving the seller a deal, make sure to help the seller while seeking to help yourself.

THE PENULTIMATE WHOLESALING GOAL: SEEK TO HELP YOUR SELLER AS YOU SEEK TO HELP YOURSELF

If you look through Book 1, you will see its insistence on ethical behavior (in the section on legal and illegal aspects of wholesaling). This section echoes the ethical lessons taught in that section.

Too many wholesalers only care about making money and finalizing deals as quickly as possible before moving on to the next one. This is regardless of whether they burn bridges with the seller/buyer or not; to them, nothing matters more than making some bucks. In many instances, such wholesalers fail to experience real success.

A wholesaler with the utmost professionalism works his or her hardest to not only make money but also build a reputation and build bridges. They know that there is nothing more powerful than an endorsement from sellers they have dealt with. When you deal fairly with a motivated seller who is under pressure to sell, he or she will remember and endorse you every chance he or she gets.

Understanding and Sympathizing With the Motivated Seller

Motivated sellers are rarely on a winning streak. Usually, they are facing hardships that are severe enough to prompt them into selling their house. This is why your penultimate goal, even as you seek to make money, is to help them. The question you might have is; how do you do that?

Earning the seller's trust

As a wholesaler, you must earn the seller's trust. Most wholesalers will assure the seller that they are purchasing the house themselves. However, it might be a better idea to tell the motivated seller what is really going on:

1) Tell the motivated seller that your specialty is solving problems for sellers who need to sell quickly.

2) Tell the seller that you have the resources to HELP them and the necessary contacts to make a quick close.

3) Tell the seller that you will do your best to find a genuine and willing buyer. Do not make the mistake so many amateurs make: that of telling the seller that a sale will undoubtedly come through. Let the seller know that while you hold your sales ability in high regard, it is quite possible that the house will not sell before the purchase contract expires.

4) However, even as you are doing your best, to be honest, and straightforward, make sure not to confuse the seller. Tell the seller to trust you and your way of doing things. Do not expose too much of your avenues; you want to seem as invulnerable as possible without being dishonest about it so that the seller can have maximum trust in you.

Assuming that you've succeeded in getting the seller to trust you and have landed a deal, next, we will focus on how to market the contract that's in your hands to increase the likelihood of selling.

MARKETING WHOLESALE PROPERTY DEALS WITH PROSPECTIVE INVESTORS

The number one reason why you and many other wholesalers may find it hard to close wholesaling deals is overpricing your deals

Imagine you have succeeded at getting a house under contract. You are excited and nervous at the same time, and you understand that it's of paramount importance that you close the deal not just because you intend to make money off it, but because you took on the responsibility of getting the job done and are determined to see it through. You know that the seller is relying on you and you want to do everything in your power to cause a few problems as possible.

Pricing Your Deal Too High and Reasons Why You May Do This

This is mostly the major reason why so many wholesalers, especially those new to the business, fail to find a buyer for their deal. You best believe that every house flipper or cash buyer you approach know that you stand to make money from the deal and that the price you offer him or her is higher than the one you offered the seller.

For the most part, they are okay with you trying to make some coin but when the pricing gets absurd, they will turn your nose up to it (you will also draw a similar reaction, by default this time, if every property you have to offer is terrible or always comes with a batch of problems).

Let us examine some reasons why you may feel compelled to overprice your deal or may otherwise overprice your wholesale deal unknowingly.

1: You overestimate your ARV (After Repair Value)

This is often a problem for wholesalers who are working with limited information (also known as wholesalers who insist they do not need many photographs for accurate number crunching, later on). It is also a problem for wholesalers who do not have similar properties on the market for apt comparison. Some wholesalers also act from a place of too much optimism, which is frankly the silliest reason out of the three given in this paragraph. Regardless, every time your ARV is too high, it will follow that you will price your deal too high in turn.

Here is how you can avoid this:

a) Always ensure that for every property you are trying to wholesale, you have similar properties to compare with. Do all you can to find a close match: trawl the web, make phone calls, or drive for dollars if you must.

b) Ensure you have sufficient data from which to estimate your ARV. You can ensure this by arming yourself with lots of photographs that show every angle of the property.

c) Make sure you have recent data to work from. This guide recommendation is that the data you are using be no more than three months old. This is why this book insists on you visiting the property, taking lots of photographs, and asking the seller questions that will guide you to his or her true reasons for wanting to sell.

Here is something else to keep in mind: if you have a tendency to conduct wishful thinking while on business, something often motivated by a desire to make even more money on your deals, you will be better off dumping this trait. Do not play mental games with yourself thinking that because your property has an attractive mural drawing on one of the bedroom walls, you can ask for an extra $5,000 in comparison to what similar properties are going for. Real estate never works this way.

2: You underestimate the rehab work necessary

This one is also all too common. This one is often a result of inexperience in rehab work and determination of repair costs. Sometimes, it is also a result of wishful thinking on the wholesaler's part.

Experienced wholesalers have admitted to routine amazement from the numbers given for repair costs on some wholesale deals they come across. Some of them have admitted to "just going ahead and doubling the amount mentioned for repairs."

Once you underestimate the costs of the rehab work necessary, it follows that you will give an overpriced figure for property in worse shape than you believe it is.

Do you want to know the best way to have an accurate feel for the cost of repairs? Well, ask an experienced real estate investor—you should have several connections by now; he or she will let you know. If you can especially speak to an experienced house flipper, doing so will do you much good. If you cannot find one you can take to lunch and ask questions, your next best option is a contractor. It's wise to find a contractor who has worked for multiple investors (think landlords, house flippers, and the like). Such contractors have their hand on the pulse on repair costs since they are actively involved in the repairs themselves.

3: Your asking wholesale fee is too high

If there ever was a hard and fast rule that ensured longevity in the wholesale business, it is this: ***Do not be greedy.***

At times, you will be tempted to ask for the world because you feel like you spent ages finding the deal and deserve a hefty reward for your troubles. It will be foolhardy to allow emotional rationalization to affect your pricing. The thing to note here is that you want people begging for your deals. You want house flippers calling you constantly to ask if you have anything in your pipeline. The last thing you want is people looking at you as a person who is constantly insulting their intelligence.

It may be difficult for you eat some humble pie and lower your overpriced figure but doing so may be utterly necessary. Even then, there are flippers and cash buyers who would have been willing to buy it at the lower price, if you had priced it that way from the very beginning, who will ignore the lowered price and shun your deals altogether. Avoid greed and always try to price your wholesale fee reasonably.

In the next chapter, we will be looking at real estate laws and what you need to be aware of as you wholesale property.

FOUR THINGS EVERY WHOLESALER SHOULD UNDERSTAND ABOUT REAL ESTATE LAWS

This section continues your education on the legal aspect of wholesaling and real estate. It is necessary that you learn as much as you can about real estate law because the truth is that the more you know about it, the less susceptible you are to breaking it and having to pay costly fines for your mistakes.

Here are four things that as a wholesaler, you ought to understand about real estate laws:

1: In some jurisdictions, the tenant has right of first refusal

When it comes to rental properties, wholesaling is at times not as simple and direct as it is when dealing with residential property. In some jurisdictions, if you are interested in wholesaling a property, you MUST give the tenants who occupy the property the opportunity to match the selling price and purchase the property. Sure enough, this is not something that applies everywhere in the U.S. but some localities demand it.

When dealing with rental property, ensure you are completely familiar with how the law works in your area of interest and whether the Tenant's Right of First Refusal applies in that particular jurisdiction. An attorney will you make sure you are compliant with the rules in place.

2: If you download any forms from the internet, have your local attorney review them before using them

This nugget of advice applies to the forms provided in this book even though they will be as valid as can be. Why is this necessary? Real estate law tends to vary, sometimes greatly, from one jurisdiction to the next. For instance, some jurisdictions will insist on certain languages for certain contracts. Here is an example that depicts what we mean by this:

Many wholesalers love wholesaling leases with the option to buy. This is fine in multiple jurisdictions until you get to Maryland. In Maryland, a lease option MUST mention "THIS IS NOT A CONTRACT TO BUY." If the form does not include this particular "language," any individual involved who did not draft the contract has the right to void it at any time. A lot of the time, this means you will be on the losing end. It is therefore vital to have a local attorney go through your downloaded contract forms to see if they adhere to local law.

If you want, you can skip the downloading bit and use forms drafted by a local attorney specializing in real estate. This will cost you a little bit of money, but that is money well spent because it will ensure your maximum protection.

3: Actual consideration needs to get paid for earnest money deposits & assignments

What does this mean? Well, when you put up a property contract as a wholesaler, you need to pay an "earnest money deposit." Book 1 covers this. An earnest money deposit shows that you and the seller have a deal in place. It serves as evidence of the existence of a real deal between the wholesaler and the seller, thus giving legal credence to all other relative proceedings that develop.

However, problems often arise when the wholesaler and the seller decide to go the "lawyer fee way," by having a nominal fee of, say, $1 or $10 stand in for the requisite earnest money deposit. The thing here is this; a lawyer is a professional, schooled formally in the facets of his or her profession. His schooling guarantees that you cannot exploit or unfairly treat him unless he or she wills it. If the lawyer sees it fit to accept an upfront fee of just $1, the court is alright with it as long as the fee is present whatever it is.

However, unlike the attorney, your seller will not be a legal professional 99% of the time and a court of equity will be compelled to step in if it determines that you are not handling the contract on serious term or there is unfair treatment of the seller. If you pay your seller $10 or even $50 as your earnest money deposit for property that may sell for $70,000, you are begging the equity court to void your contract and being more than a little unprofessional.

Do not be cheap, which means you should never insist on paying a minimal amount. Recall that this book has already insisted that your penultimate goal is to help your motivated seller even as you seek to make money. There often needs to be sufficient consideration money paid to prove that indeed, the deal is real.

4: A title attorney or title company that works with wholesalers is a necessity

No, this does not mean you should set up a fake title company or hire a stand-in title attorney as a smokescreen just because the law asks it. Many wholesalers do this and it eventually comes back to haunt them.

Here is why you need to work with a title company, or at least a title attorney that specializes in working with wholesalers:

As a wholesaler, the motivated buyer is your no. 1 target. In most cases, this automatically means the bulk of properties you are going after are distressed properties that have underlying issues prompting their sale. Each distressed property will likely come with its own unique batch of problems, distressed people, and circumstances.

It could be that the person selling the property is masquerading as the real owner. It could be that there are aliens on the property who have refused to leave the property for years and you do not know about it. You could be dealing with a case of a missing heir or multiple unknown heirs who lay claim to the property.

Best believe that these issues only compound when you attempt to sell off these distressed properties. If you employ a title company or a title attorney, they will help you navigate such issues and warn you if they think the situation warrants pulling the plug.

Let's take the legal discussion a bit further.

A FURTHER EXAMINATION OF THE LEGAL AND ILLEGAL ASPECTS OF WHOLESALING

In this section, we shall outline foolproof strategies that will help you keep on the right side of things as a wholesaler:

Building on Book 1's coverage of the same topic, this section—as was the case in book 1—covers some legal elements of wholesaling. This is important because of way too many wholesalers, especially those relatively new to the business, often get themselves into trouble with the law because they jump straight into wholesaling without necessarily understanding if some of the things they do are legal or not.

With regard to the legal side of things, Book 1 concentrates on the ethics of business: which factors qualify your wholesaling deal as either ethical or unethical regardless of the purity of your intentions. Book 1 mentions dealing with naïve or low-income sellers as unethical and thus, illegal. □

Certainly, it would be unreasonable for your State to demand that you only deal with high-income sellers; the State knows this. However, depending on how you hammer the deal out (with buying at a very low price and proceeding to sell high as an example), the state could find you guilty and penalize you heavily.

This section builds upon Book 1's ethical business coverage (chapter 2), even as it focuses away from it and onto the more technical aspects (meaning that the content here is in no way a substitute for what you learned in book 1. You still have to tend to business ethics first). By saying this section shall concentrate on the "more technical aspects," we primarily mean the brokering issue.

You could be as ethical as ever, you could do business the right way and painstakingly build your portfolio the way a serious wholesaler would and the State could still criminalize your activity and slap you with a penalty on an illegal brokering charge.

Read on to understand this.

The Legality of Wholesaling

Many people who want to put you off wholesaling—usually for their own personal reasons—will repeatedly bash the legality of wholesaling and do all they can to make it seem as if the entire practice is skating on the edge of legality in every aspect of it. Some criticism is valid especially seeing how wholesalers all over the US, with Ohio based ones making up most of the numbers, have had to pay fines for "illegal practices." However, the legality (or lack of) of wholesaling is often exaggerated and there is a lot of nonsense floating around.

Let us determine clearly what is illegal and what is all right for you to do.

What Is Illegal About Wholesaling? The Brokering Issue

The essence of the "is wholesaling really legal?" argument 100% revolves around one term *"brokering."* Different states define the broker in different ways but generally, a broker is the person who helps put a deal together.

Let us delve a bit deeper into this and use Florida's in-depth definition of what a broker is as an example:

Florida states, 'Broker' refers to:

"An individual who, for another individual, and for a compensation or some other valuable consideration, directly or indirectly promised or paid, expressly or impliedly, or with intent to collect or receive a compensation or a valuable consideration, therefore, appraises auctions, sells, exchanges, purchases, rents or offers...to appraise, negotiate the sale or auction the sale, purchase or exchange property...or any interest that concerns the same."

While this definition is longwinded, it drives the point home. Which brings us to this: the people who argue that wholesaling is illegal do so on the claim that the wholesaler is acting in a "broker's capacity" without possessing a license to act in that particular capacity.

A further bump in the situation

To complicate our situation further, there is the problematic issue of "marketing" a property you are not in ownership of. Most states in the U.S insist that "marketing property" qualifies as brokering. Let us go back to our story in Book 1, about James the wholesaler getting a call from Nora the seller, signing a purchase contract with her, assigning the contract to his friend Joe the house flipper and making $5,000 in wholesale fees at the end of it all.

If James did not have Joe as a valuable contact and had put the house up on, say, Craigslist, would he have been marketing Nora's property? You bet he would have! But then again, what if he was not really marketing the property? What defines marketing in the first place? Looking back at our story, do James' approach of Joe, the cash buyer, and house flipper qualify as marketing? If you were to pose this question to 10 different licensed lawyers, you may very well get ten different answers and leave even more confused than before.

What is our take on this? It is indeed true that the way most wholesalers work has illegal elements to it.

Illegal wholesaling

When you put a deal under contract (see purchase agreement) going ahead and telling the world about it on Craigslist and related sites, then going ahead to assign the deal (see assignment agreement) will no doubt get you slapped with a state government fine along with a misdemeanor charge.

What you can do

This chapter will show you several strategies to apply to ensure you do not run afoul of the law. However, always lead your every wholesaling activity with this:

"How comfortable am I if I have to defend my position if my local real estate commission starts asking questions?"

Strategies to Apply to Ensure You Wholesale "The Right Way"

Here are the promised strategies:

1) Get your license: This one does not need too much examination. Nobody will accuse you that you are brokering without the required license if you already

have a license. It may cost you $2,000 but this is far better than having to pay a State penalty for breaking the law.

2) Buy the property and then proceed to sell it: Note that you do not have to do this but it is effective. This way, when you do market your property in whatever capacity you choose to, nobody will accuse you of breaking any law or brokering in any sort of way.

Wholesaling and the Law

The truth is that there is no one answer as far as the legality of wholesaling is concerned. If you do not care about how close to the line you skate, wholesaling is a nice way to make money.

However, to ensure you are operating a wholesaling business that is pure and as solidly legal as it gets, the best strategy that will save you lots of money—in having to buy the property outright before selling it or having to pay a State fine at some point down the line—is to *get your broker's license.* This way, you will completely shut down any claims that you are "brokering without the required license".

In the next chapter, we will be discussing how to conduct contract assignment in the right way.

CONDUCTING CONTRACT ASSIGNMENT THE RIGHT WAY FOR EXAMPLE CONTRACTS EVERY WHOLESALER NEEDS

By now, you may have sat through enough get-rich-quick pitches to know that when it comes to wholesaling, contract assignment is extremely vital. The get-rich-quick gurus do contract assignment introductions all the time, only they never take you through the process as well as all the necessary contracts you need. This section will show you what these "gurus" mean when they say, "You stand to make $5,000 in 30 days via wholesaling contract assignment."

In which scenario will contract assignment be necessary?

We'll keep this simple and terse since Book 1 covers this particular bit competently. A contract assignment will be necessary *"when you find a property owner who is willing to sell their property below its market value. You will then resell the property to another person, often another real estate investor at a higher price."* A contract assignment has the seller commit to selling to you and once he or she puts down a signature, he or she cannot change his or her mind or opt to sell to another person behind your back.

How Does Contract Assignment Work Exactly?

Here is how contract assignment work:

Step 1: Find a motivated seller

We have already explored the concept of the motivated seller. To add some more body to it, a motivated seller is somebody who NEEDS to sell his or her property because of some distress or other aspects of life that precipitates the sale of the property.

Understand that there is a massive disparity between wanting to sell and needing to sell. When an individual "wants" to sell, it is likely that there is no real sense of urgency. The seller may say something like, "I'm curious to see what this house goes for in the current market, since I may well need to sell next year." This sort of fellow is not a motivated seller. On the other hand, somebody who "needs" to sell is often conducting a running battle against time and is likely to say something like, "I have to sell my property ASAP as I am moving back to Alabama to nurse my ailing father."

Step 2: Get an assignment contract signed by both you and the seller

Multiple assignment contracts are available on the internet (and this book will give you several you can photocopy and use.) However, and this very book has insisted on it in a previous section, you need to ensure a local attorney goes through your contract template to ensure it's in line with the laws in your particular jurisdiction.

Both you and the seller need to sign the assignment contract. This contract, in addition to having the seller commit to only selling to you, empowers you to "assign" the purchase to a 3rd party, and as you well understand by now, your wholesaling career will make absolutely no sense without the presence of this 3rd party.

Step 3: Submit the contract to title

This process tends to differ by state. Still, there is not much by way of intricacies or complexities. Whichever state you operate from, you deal with a closing attorney or a title company. Most states will let you choose whomever you fancy dealing with. Take care to understand the stipulations of your state regarding this.

The Title Company or closing attorney will conduct a title search to verify that the seller is a valid one. The title search checks the property's historical records—to ensure there are no "aliens" on the property—and a host of other things. If the title company concludes that the property has a "defective title," which essentially means that the ownership of the property is not straightforward and complicates any buying/selling procedures, it is wise to let the property go and look for something else.

The title search is a necessary process because most distressed properties often have a lot of baggage. Do not be one of those wholesalers who are too cheap or too impatient to see this process through or someone who is too foolish to understand that a title search is only in place to protect them.

Step 4: Find a buyer and assign the contract assignment to him/her

As you get started out in this business, finding a buyer may be quite daunting. However, you will get one eventually, provided the property you have on your hands is not so bad to a point of being unsellable. When you get a buyer, you can then begin your process of completing the transaction and the whole business altogether. Assign the contract to the buyer and sign a purchase agreement to finalize everything.

However, how do you ensure that your buyer is actually serious? How do you ensure that he or she is not just poking around for a prospective property that he or she "could buy some unspecified time in the future when the money or circumstances are right?" To ensure you are dealing with a solid buyer, you should insist on a non-refundable "earnest money deposit" fee.

Having the buyer furnish this amount will solidify your position as far as making a profit goes. It does not matter if the buyer ends up buying the property or backs out at the last moment; this money will remain yours. This amount may be as much or as little as you require; just keep it reasonable and you will be fine. (Most wholesalers prefer several hundreds of dollars, but some seasoned ones will ask for as much as $5,000). When the buyer deposits this amount, you can be sure that he or she is interested in buying the property.

NOTE: Your title company or closing attorney will hold this fee until the completion of the transaction/deal or until the buyer backs out.

Step 5: Get Paid

This is the wholesaler's favorite part. You will typically make your money/get paid once the end buyer wires the funds for your deal. As outlined before, this money will cover the amount you agreed with the original property seller as well as your amount for facilitating the whole thing (wholesale fee).

Examples of Necessary Contracts Every Wholesaler Needs

As stated earlier, you need several contracts as you embark on wholesaling. The most important ones you need are:

Sample Assignment Contract

This is a sample assignment contract you can tweak and make yours. Remember to have an attorney look it over to ensure its regality in your state (do this for all the contracts here)

Agreement for Sale Contract

To ensure you get a contract that is nicely formatted, you can download one from this link:

https://www.dropbox.com/s/d87nyy7ql4k9t21/AGREEMENT%20FOR%20SALE%20Contract.doc?dl=0:

Sample Purchase Agreement 1

This link has a customizable sample purchase agreement:

https://www.dropbox.com/s/8zbytogz50eeanl/Purchase%20and%20Sale%20Agreement.doc?dl=0

Sample Purchase Agreement 2

This link has another customizable purchase agreement:

https://www.dropbox.com/sh/diqx90c07ens4hj/AACod1W4GpyOoNGype59RvRaa?dl=0

Sample Purchase Agreement 3

This link has a standard purchase and sale agreement:

https://www.dropbox.com/s/3wo95rel7ylgn98/Standard%20Purchase%20and%20Sale%20Agreement.doc?dl=0

Option to Purchase Agreement

Here is a sample option to purchase agreement:

https://www.dropbox.com/s/admnnk2pa827ky3/Option%20to%20Purchase%20Agreement.doc?dl=0

Option to Purchase (Flex Option) Agreement

https://www.dropbox.com/s/yol7f6oqx47gqqc/Option%20t o%20Purchase%20Real%20Estate%20Agreement.doc?dl=0 has another option to purchase agreement that you can customize

To take it even a bit further, here (https://www.dropbox.com/s/qc3tqw7n2whc8sn/Sample% 20Contract%20Assignment%20with%20Specific%20Details .doc?dl=0) is a sample contract assignment with specific details, dates, and monetary figures.

You can download the templates from this link:

https://www.dropbox.com/sh/diqx90c07ens4hj/AACod1W 4GpyOoNGype59RvRaa?dl=0

Last but not least, we will discuss something very critical in wholesaling.

Your Seller Lead Sheet: What to Say When Your Phone Rings and There's a Customer on the Line

You know what a motivated seller is and even more importantly, you know how to seek out their business. If you follow everything outlined in this book, there will come a time when you have no problems drawing in customers and pushing multiple deals.

With this said, what do you do when the big moment arrives and the phone rings with a motivated seller on the line? You may be asking yourself any of the following questions:

1. What shall I say to the customer?

2. How do I conduct myself so that I inspire confidence in him or her?

3. What are the questions that I should ask?

4. What will come next even if I do everything right?

This section will help you not just assess incoming real estate seller leads, but turn them into viable opportunities:

1: Remember that a motivated seller requires your help often more than you need his/hers.

When a motivated seller goes out of her way to call you, it is usually the case that she needs your help and would appreciate it if you helped her move her property as fast as possible. This is why the first thing to do before picking up your phone is to breathe deeply and calm yourself down. If you are nervous and shifty and the motivated seller, who may possess the very same emotions, catches on, she will lose her confidence in you from the start and immediately consider seeking out somebody else.

Just relax, breathe deeply, and pick up your phone. If a motivated seller is on the line, something you will know soon enough by her attitude and particular situation, you will have a deal in little time. Otherwise, if it is not a motivated seller on the line, bid them goodbye and hang up. Many new wholesalers make the mistake of trying to convince a seller to make a fast sale. As a wholesaler, remember that your job is not to create urgency; your job is to act upon present urgency in your seller.

2: With the pleasantries covered, employ a set of questions on the seller

Not only will this help you keep the conversation going, and thus put the seller at ease, it will also help you glean vital information about the seller so that you have a clear picture on who you are dealing with.

Here are the things to ask about:

1. The details of the property for sale (number of bathrooms, bedrooms, address Etc.)

2. The primary reason for selling

3. What he or she believes the house is worth at least based on similar sales in their neighborhood

4. The asking price, if they already have one in mind, and whether they would consider lowering it

5. The repairs and rehab activities the house needs

It is vital to remember that you should not take a seller's word as fact until you have visited the house. A distressed seller eager to sell quickly may exaggerate some things and gloss over others. Still, never underestimate the importance of building rapport. Humans tend to do business with other humans they like. Rather than sound too formal or professional, be warm and walk the customer through your questions as you would an old friend. In other words, be casual all through.

3: Assess the customer's need level

As you walk the customer through your questions, pay great attention to the signals he or she sends:

1. What is the true reason behind the sale?

2. Is the need immediate?

3. How much money are they really looking for?

Getting answers to these questions will greatly help you understand whether you want to go ahead with the deal on the table or not. If, for instance, your customer starts talking about all the recent upgrades made to their house, understand that such a seller stands a better chance of getting top dollar with an agent and politely end the conversation.

4: A confident person will speak directly and give confident answers

This bit will glue together everything else on this section and determine the level of success you have in inspiring the seller's confidence. Many wholesalers concern themselves with whether (or not) they will come across as nervous. Will the customer detect nervousness or inexperience?

A simple strategy to exude both confidence and professionalism is to speak in a calm voice. Keep your words plain as well. When your answers are short, simple, and straight to the point, you will usually sound like a person who knows his business.

For example, let us assume that you've found direct mail to be the best approach to generating leads and the seller asks how you got their name. Your best answer would be, "I purchased an address list based on tax records."

The seller could as well ask about your particular interest in his or her property. You do not need to make your answer complicated or use too many words to try to impress. You may simply say, "I purchase houses in my neighborhood and rehabilitate them. After I am through with that, I either sell them or rent them out." This is a simple yet honest answer.

Most property owners understand that rehabilitating and selling off properties is something some real estate investors do. However, avoid describing yourself as an "investor." It may come across as entitled and lacking in humility.

5: Do not be afraid to ask for a little time if you need it

Many wholesalers assume that they have to know the answers to everything upfront. It is not your job to know everything even though it helps to be knowledgeable. If the customer asks you a question and you are unsure of the correct answer, just let such a customer know you will seek out the necessary information and call back with an answer. Again, keep it simple and be calm. A lot of the time, calm and simple is all you need to gain your customer's trust.

CONCLUSION

We have come to the end of the book. Thank you for reading and congratulations on reading until the end.

At this point, you can call yourself a competent wholesaler. Both Book 1 and this one have done a superb job of showing you how to conduct business as a pro wholesaler. There is a fair share of unconventional advice within, and it is my recommendation that you take everything here to heart.

Remember that wholesaling is something anyone can do. It does not matter whether you have a million dollars in the bank or not; it does not matter if your family has a track record of real estate success or not; all that matters is that you are willing to put in the work. This book guides you steadily- by getting to this point, you have already learned all the important elements of wholesaling. You are ready to be a successful wholesaler.

However, with wholesaling being such a vast topic, it is impossible for two books to cover everything. You will still need to glean as much as you can from other sources. However, this book is more than good enough as a spine for your wholesaling education.

If you found the book valuable, can you recommend it to others? One way to do that is to post a review on Amazon.

Please leave a review for this book on Amazon!

Thank you and good luck!

Get Your Free Copy of

How to be a Real Estate Millionaire

To Get Your Free Copy, Open the Link

https://ebraveboy_3ee2.gr8.com/

www.ingramcontent.com/pod-product-compliance
Lightning Source LLC
Chambersburg PA
CBHW071209220526
45468CB00002B/556